'A' Level Revision Notes – When Will The

'A' LEVEL REV NOTES FOR KATE ATKINSON'S 'WHEN WILL THERE BE GOOD NEWS' - Study guide (page-by-page analysis)

by Joe Broadfoot

All rights reserved

Copyright © Joe Broadfoot, 2016

The right of Joe Broadfoot to be identified as the author of this work has been asserted in accordance with Section 77 of the Copyright, Designs and Patents

ISBN-13: 978-1537283807

ISBN-10: 1537283804

'A' Level Revision Notes – When Will There Be Good News

CONTENTS

INTRODUCTION: 4

CRITERIA: 5

ESSAY PLANNING: 6

CHAPTER 1: 9

CHAPTER 2: 13

CHAPTER 3: 15

CHAPTER 4: 23

CHAPTER 5: 29

CHAPTER 6: 31

CHAPTER 7: 35

CHAPTER 8: 39

CHAPTER 9: 42

CHAPTER 10: 47

CHAPTER 11: 48

CHAPTER 12: 52

CHAPTER 13: 53

CHAPTER 14: 56

CHAPTER 15: 59

CHAPTER 16: 60

CHAPTER 17: 63

CHAPTER 18: 64

'A' Level Revision Notes – When Will There Be Good News

CHAPTER 19: 67

CHAPTER 20: 68

CHAPTER 21: 69

CHAPTER 22: 71

CHAPTER 23: 75

CHAPTER 24: 76

CHAPTER 25: 79

CHAPTER 26: 81

CHAPTER 27: 83

CHAPTER 28: 85

CHAPTER 29: 89

CHAPTER 30: 92

CHAPTER 31: 94

CHAPTER 32: 95

CHAPTER 33: 97

CHAPTER 34: 99

CHAPTER 35: 101

CHAPTER 36: 102

CHAPTER 37: 104

CHAPTER 38: 106

CHAPTER 39: 108

CHAPTER 40: 109

CHAPTER 41: 110

GLOSSARY: 111

'A' Level Revision Notes – When Will There Be Good News
Introduction

This textbook is designed for students studying Kate Atkinson's 'When Will There Be Good News' at 'A' level. Useful quotations are selected and each page is analysed to provide students with a useful study guide to accompany the original text.

'A' Level Revision Notes – When Will There Be Good News

Criteria for high marks

Make sure you use appropriate critical language (see glossary of literary terms at the back). You need your argument to be fluent, well-structured and coherent. Stay focused!

Analyse and explore the use of form, structure and the language. Explore how these aspects affect the meaning.

Make connections between texts and look at different interpretations. Explore their strengths and weaknesses. Don't forget to use supporting references to strengthen your argument.

Analyse and explore the context.

Best essay practice

There are so many way to write an essay. Many schools use **PEE** for paragraphs: point/evidence/explain. Others use **PETER**: point/evidence/technique/explain/reader; **PEEL**: point, example, explain, link; **PEEE**: point/evidence/explain/explore. Whichever method you use, make sure you mention the **writer's effects**. This generally is what most students forget to add. You must think of what the writer is trying to achieve by using a particular technique and what is actually achieved. Do not just spot techniques and note them. You may get some credit for using appropriate technology, but unless you can comment on the effect created on the reader and/or the writer's intention, you will miss out on most of the marks available.

'A' Level Revision Notes – When Will There Be Good News
Essay planning

In order to write a good essay it is necessary to plan. In fact, it is best to quite formulaic in an exam situation, as you won't have much time to get started. Therefore I will ask you to learn the following acronym: **DATMC (Definition, Application, Terminology, Main, Conclusion**. Some schools call it: **GSLMC (General, Specific, Link, Main, Conclusion)**, but it amounts to the same thing. The first three letters concern the introduction. (Of course, the alternative is to leave some blank lines and write your introduction after you have completed the main body of your essay, but it is probably not advisable for most students).

Let us first look at the following exam question, which is on poetry (of course, the same essay-planning principles apply to essays on novels and plays as well).

QUESTION: Explore how the poet conveys **feelings** in the poem.

STEP ONE: Identify the **keyword** in the question. (I have already done this, by highlighting it in **bold**). If you are following GSLMC, you now need to make a **general statement** about what feelings are. Alternatively, if you're following DATMC, simply **define** 'feelings'. For example, 'Feelings are emotion states or reactions or vague, irrationals ideas and beliefs'.

STEP TWO: If you are following GSLMC, you now need to make a **specific statement** linking feelings (or whatever else you've defined) to how they appear in the poem.

'A' Level Revision Notes – When Will There Be Good News

Alternatively, if you're following DATMC, simply define which 'feelings' **apply** in this poem. For example, 'The feelings love, fear and guilt appear in this poem, and are expressed by the speaker in varying degrees.'

STEP THREE: If you are following GSLMC, you now need to make a **link statement** identifying the methods used to convey the feelings (or whatever else you've defined) in the poem. Alternatively, if you're following DATMC, simply define which **techniques** are used to convey 'feelings' in this poem. For example, 'The poet primarily uses alliteration to emphasise his heightened emotional state, while hyperbole and enjambment also help to convey the sense that the speaker is descending into a state of madness.

STEP FOUR: Whether you are following GSLMC or DATMC, the next stage is more or less the same. The main part of the essay involves writing around **six paragraphs**, using whichever variation of PEEE you prefer. In my example, I will use **Point, Evidence, Exploration, Effect** on the listener. To make your essay even stronger, try to use your quotations chronologically. It will be easier for the examiner to follow, which means you are more likely to achieve a higher grade. To be more specific, I recommend that you take and analyse two quotations from the beginning of the poem, two from the middle, and two at the end.

STEP FIVE: Using Carol Ann Duffy's poem, 'Stealing', here's an example of how you could word one of your six paragraphs: **(POINT)** 'Near the beginning of the poem, the speaker's determination is expressed.' **(EVIDENCE)** 'This is achieved through the words: 'Better off dead than giving in'.

'A' Level Revision Notes – When Will There Be Good News
(EXPLORATION). The use of 'dead' emphasizes how far the speaker is prepared to go in pursuit of what he wants, although there is a sense that he is exaggerating (hyperbole). **(EFFECT)** The listener senses that the speaker may be immature given how prone he is to exaggerate his own bravery.

STEP SIX: After writing five or more paragraphs like the one above, it will be time to write a **conclusion**. In order to do that, it is necessary to sum up your previous points and evaluate them. This is not the time to introduce additional quotations. Here is an example of what I mean: 'To conclude, the poet clearly conveys the speaker's anger. Although the listener will be reluctant to completely sympathise with a thief, there is a sense that the speaker is suffering mentally, which makes him an interesting and partially a sympathetic character. By using a dramatic monologue form, the poet effectively conveys the speaker's mental anguish, which makes it easier to more deeply understand what first appears to be inexplicable acts of violence.

'A' Level Revision Notes – When Will There Be Good News

Part I: In The Past

Chapter 1: Harvest

The title suggests something will come to fruition or that it is Autumn. That time setting suggests that crops will be cut down or harvested.

The first words are 'The heat', which is more indicative of summer, and we are informed that is 'oppressive' for the mother of 8-year-old Jessica, 6-year-old Joanna and baby Joseph (17). 'Like the maze at Hampton Court', they feel 'trapped' (17). We can only assume it is a family crisis, through the setting's inevitable associations with Henry VIII. We discover that 'the lane' snakes 'one way and then another' (17). The language tells us nothing feels safe and secure in this environment.

Jessica, holding the dog's lead, seems in control, while Joanna doesn't 'want to think for herself', so seems to have opted to be a follower rather than a leader (18). The mother, Gabrielle, swears, so she is clearly frustrated at their father's choice of an 'idyll' in the 'country' (18). Her name implies she is angelic, like the Angel Gabriel, at least in comparison to their father, the famous writer Howard Mason, who has 'driven' off in the

'A' Level Revision Notes – When Will There Be Good News

family car (18).

We feel some sympathy for their plight, particularly as the family have not adjusted to their new surroundings in Devon (19). Joanna misses Wonder Woman and the Beano comic, which suggests the time setting is around the 1970s.

We are taken back in time. Tensions erupt, as Gabrielle hurls a jug at Howard after accusing him of smelling of 'failure' (20).

The perfume 'Je Reviens' seems significant as it is repeated, and in French it means 'I return' (20, 19). This hints that characters may do the same. Even Howard could do the same, although he has another lover in London. The writer leaves the reader guessing, offering little explanation.

Regardless of that, his departure appears to have destroyed his family, particularly Gabrielle, who has still not taken up painting again despite his absence. She seems absorbed with bitterness, spitting out the word 'poet' when describing Howard's 'other woman' (21).

Nevertheless, Gabrielle is portrayed as a plucky single mother, when she claims 'we are not downhearted'

'A' Level Revision Notes – When Will There Be Good News

despite the family members looking 'like refugees' (22).

The reader feels even more sympathy upon hearing that Joseph can't 'shake off a summer cold' (22). Likewise, more sympathy is aroused for Joanna in particular, as her allergies start to flare up, and we discover she suffers from 'bad luck', as Joseph has inherited his mother's dark hair and pale skin, while Jessica has her green eyes and 'painter's hands' (22). Later, we'll discover the irony in that statement about Jo's supposed ill-luck.

We begin to see the action more and more through Joanna's perspective, as we sense that she admires her mother and older sister, Jessica, for being 'fierce' (23). Although, it is a **third-person narrative**, the use of **free indirect speech** heightens our identification with Jo.

The writer builds up a sense of foreboding when Gabrielle says they'll be 'harvesting' the wheat, 'cutting it down' (24). It appears to be a rather violent way of expressing a harvest.

We discover that Gabrielle 'eloped' with their father and thereby missed out on her inheritance. She followed her

'A' Level Revision Notes – When Will There Be Good News

heart and is now paying the price. The reader feels sympathy for her plight.

The pace of the narrative quickens as the family dog is kicked 'so hard' that it flies through the air, landing 'in the wheat' (26). The perpetrator is a man, 'making a funny huffing, puffing noise' (26). Suspense is added by him appear to grow 'bigger all the time' as he pursues them (26).

Gabrielle is 'cut down' like wheat and and blood covers 'her strawberry dress' (27). Joanna assumes Jessica has been 'stabbed' too, but gains a modicum of security from 'being lost in the wheat', which has already closed around her sister 'like a golden blanket' (27). Ironically, Joanna is supposed to be plagued with bad luck, but here she is emerging unscathed from the attack with 'not a scratch' on her (28).

Thirty years later, at the age of 36, Joanna cannot 'remember' the name of the dog. The reader can empathise with her traumatic experience, which may have caused memory loss (28).

'A' Level Revision Notes – When Will There Be Good News

Part II: Today

Chapter 2: Flesh and Blood

The title of the chapter ties in with the themes of family bloodshed, which are apparent at the end of the last chapter.

↳ *adds to the fact that a reader will think Jackson is the criminal.*

We see the Yorkshire Dales as a great expanse of greenery from the perspective of a Yorkshireman, a second **focaliser**, who is unfamiliar with this part of the county, and its 'alien corn' (31).

He is trying to blend in 'better', which indicates he's been unsuccessful in the past (32). The reader wonders who he is and why he is there.

Slowly, we find out more information. He has an expensive 'gold Breitling' watch, given to him by a female (33). The writer is adding suspense and mystery, by adding questions rather than answers to the narrative.

His 'army' style undercover mission appears to be macabre, as we discover his target is 'Nat', a small boy 'with dark eyes and black curls' (34). The reader can

pedophile feeling for a reader.

'A' Level Revision Notes – When Will There Be Good News

guess he's there to kidnap the child, who is unprotected. We can sense the resentment towards the father figure in the Nat's life: 'Mr Arty-Farty. The False Dad'(34). Yet rather than kidnapping him, the man, whom we assume is the biological father, touches Nat's hair, causing him to leap back as if he has 'been scalded' (35).

'One of the mothers' is suspicious, but the man manages to make her think he is lost, evoking her sympathy, if not the reader's (36). The setting makes the scene even more threatening as the trees are 'black and skeletal' (36).

When he gets to the waterfall, the man drops the boy's 'hair' into a 'plastic bag' and the reader wonders why (37). We finally discover that the man is 'Jackson Brodie', but we can only guess his motive (37).

don't find out who he is to the end. Now don't think he is the killer from before.

14

'A' Level Revision Notes – When Will There Be Good News

Chapter 3: The Life and Adventures of Reggie Chase, Containing a Faithful Account of the Fortunes, Misfortunes, Uprisings, Downfallings and Complete Career of the Chase Family

The length of the title gives it a comic effect, as does the name Reggie Chase, the third **focaliser** in this third-person narrative. The baby behaving 'like a suicidal starfish' adds to this effect. Dr Hunter has ensured her baby's food is 'organic' and 'mashed up and frozen in little plastic tubs', so all Reggie has to do is 'warm it through in the microwave' (38). We don't know his relationship with Dr Hunter, at this stage, which builds up suspense and the reader's curiosity.

We discover that Reggie is a small sixteen-year-old girl, who looks younger but feels 'a hundred years old' inside (39). Her name, which is normally a man's name, alerts us to her unusualness.

She appears to be repelled by sexuality, partly because of her mother's behaviour with 'the Man-Who-Came-Before-Gary' and decides she will be 'quite happy to die a virgin' (40).

'A' Level Revision Notes – When Will There Be Good News

We find out that Billy is 'pretty much a career criminal', and she has 'accepted' a fake 'ID card' from him (41). Initially, we could mistakenly guess that he is a love interest of sorts to her, whether she realises it or not.

We discover from her dialogue with Dr Hunter that Reggie is Scottish, as she uses the vernacular, saying 'Och' (41). She is self-effacing although she has worked on a translation of 'some of Pliny's letters', she remains modest (41). Like 'Pliny the Younger' we expect to give an honest account of a tragedy, like Vesuvius perhaps (41).

We find out why Reggie is an 'old soul' and that her mother has 'gone'. The euphemism implies she has not got over or fully accepted her mother's death (42).

Violence does not appear far away, as we hear that Reggie 'had a puppy once but her brother threw it out of the window' (43). At this stage, we find out that the brother is Billy, who 'may be trouble' but must be forgiven according to her late mother, as 'Blood's thicker than water' (44). The reader's sympathy for Reggie increases as we find out, amongst other things, that Billy takes back the 'MacBook' he gives her for Christmas (45).

'A' Level Revision Notes – When Will There Be Good News

Nevertheless, she appears untainted by all her negative life experiences, so far. Reggie is pursuing her education, despite the odds stacked against her. We find out that she relates to 'Dickens' because his books are 'full of plucky abandoned orphans struggling to make their way in the world' (46).

From Reggie's perspective, we discover her tutor, Ms Macdonald, is terminally ill and at 'death's door' (47). The tutor is eccentric and 'too fussy' in Reggie's opinion (47). As readers, we are beginning to see cracks in Reggie's personality, as she is quite judgmental deep inside and perhaps resentful.

Reggie is immediatly set up as innocent and victim like.

She is clearly bright as she 'won a scholarship', aged twelve, but hated attending 'the horrible posh school' (48, 47). Her fees were partly paid for by the army, as her father once served in the Royal Scots before being shot by 'friendly fire' (48). The experience has given Reggie an early taste of 'irony'.

Meanwhile, Reggie's meat-eating mother is portrayed as a significantly less sensitive character, although 'the Man-Who-Came-Before-Gary' who got 'Mum to do just about anything' still could not get her to eat 'chicken' (49). We quickly get the idea that Reggie's mother has had a lot of different partners since Reggie's father's death: too many to name. This makes us feel more sorry for Reggie.

'A' Level Revision Notes – When Will There Be Good News

Nevertheless, Reggie sees her mother as 'kind', unlike Ms McDonald (50). Clearly, blood is thicker than water to Reggie, as the generous Ms McDonald is tutoring her in return for a few errands.

There is a reference to Hemingway's short story: 'A Clean, Well-Lighted Place' that follows. The repetition of the Spanish word 'nada', which means 'nothing', implies that Reggie lives in an emotional void.

Perhaps our trust in Reggie is eroded somewhat when she advises Dr Jo Hunter to 'always trust her feelings', despite the fact that she does not believe in that advice herself (51). The reader begins to think Reggie may be deceitful. Perhaps she is putting on an act.

Dr Hunter, meanwhile, is portrayed as a caring mother, who has been forced to go back to work because of 'Neil's business' hitting 'a sticky patch' (51). She is sentimental, talking to 'the dog' on the phone if the baby is asleep (52).

However, the doctor, on the surface at least, does not mourn the death of her father, who was a writer,

'A' Level Revision Notes – When Will There Be Good News

preferring to focus on the lonely death of 'the first dog in space' (53). Perhaps she is in denial.

Like Reggie, the doctor uses Latin to express herself, when she says 'Timeo Danaos et dona ferentes', which roughly translated means: 'I fear the Greeks, even those bearing gifts' (54). This refers to the notion of a Trojan horse and implies that Reggie has the power to wreak havoc on the doctor's house from her trusted position on the inside.

The doctor's husband, Mr Hunter, reveals that Joanna's 'family came from money', originally (55). This certainly sounds like the same Joanna we met in Chapter 1, who escaped the vicious attack. She is more romantic than her husband, who calls her 'home' an 'investment' (56).

Reggie compares the Hunters favourably with Ms MacDonald, whom she describes as 'slovenly' (57). This shows Reggie's judgmental side, once again.

Meanwhile, Dr Hunter is portrayed as a self-proclaimed 'all-rounder' and all her achievements are displayed on 'a big noticeboard' (58). Reggie may be slightly resentful, although she does not show it on the surface.

'A' Level Revision Notes – When Will There Be Good News

Adding mystery to the narrative, a strange woman in a 'black suit' arrives (59). The reader is intrigued, guessing it must be bad news, as black implies tragedy or that something negative is about to happen or to be revealed.

Reggie worries that the unexpected visit has something to do with 'Bad-Boy Billy', and she has to guess as she is not privy to the discussion that follows (60). From the noticeboard, Reggie knows the visitor was a chief inspector of the police. The reader's curiosity is further aroused.

Reggie hopes to spend Christmas with the Hunters rather than the Hussains, who aren't 'her family' (61). Technically, neither are the Hunters, so you get the feeling that Reggie may be deluding herself.

The baby, she helps take care of, is named 'Gabriel Joseph Hunter', presumably after Jo's mother and brother (62). He is surrounded by nautical imagery like 'sailboats', which may hint at death by drowning (62).

'A' Level Revision Notes – When Will There Be Good News

Jo and Reggie take the baby 'to a hotel near Peebles for afternoon tea' and really mean it when they say they are 'happy' (63). It reminds Reggie of how unhappy her mother was with the Man-Who-Came-Before-Gary, despite protestations to the contrary. We wonder what he did and why his name cannot be mentioned.

The focus switches back to the Hunters and the lack of evidence that Neil has ever had a 'sticky patch', given the 'lovely house, two cars' and 'fridge full of expensive food' (64). You can guess that the Hunters are living beyond their means.

Neil appears to be an unloving husband and father, behaving 'like a runner in a relay race' around the baby and like 'a getaway driver' (64, 65).

Neil is 'handsome', according to Reggie, and is 'like a comedy Glaswegian' (66). The baby likes his father 'well enough', but thinks his mother is 'a goddess' (67). Reggie's observations show how she has warmed to the family.

For a second time, 'the Heimlich manoeuvre' is mentioned, which implies the baby may choke to death (68). We also discover that Neil is much less worried

'A' Level Revision Notes – When Will There Be Good News

about the baby than his wife, as to him babies are 'virtually indestructible' (69). This makes him appear foolish and insensitive.

We guess that Reggie's mother drowned, as she imagines her 'anchored underwater by her hair' and holds her breath to imitate the sensation (70). Reggie does not tell Jo about her mother being dead, as she thinks 'the weight of the sadness' might be too much for the doctor (71). This shows how sensitive Reggie is to others. Therefore, Reggie pretends her mother is 'alive' (72).

The ominous sight of 'a blur of something black' alerts the reader that all may not be well (73). It disappears, but it is disconcerting.

Reggie hopes more and more to be invited to 'move in' with the Hunters (74). Her attachment to the family seems to be becoming dangerously close. Reggie seems to realise that despite all her platitudes about 'love', Jo is desperately sad (75). This shows how perceptive Reggie is.

'A' Level Revision Notes – When Will There Be Good News

Chapter 4: She Would Get The Flowers Herself

Chapter 4's strange title seems to indicate that the subject will be another woman wronged by a man. So far in the novel that has often been the case. However, it may be dangerous to assume that it is a man who is supposed to get the flowers for her, as perhaps it is a member of her own gender. Once again a lack of information keeps the reader guessing.

The title seems doubly strange when we discover that when shopping for her engagement ring, the loving Patrick tells the jeweller: 'This beautiful woman needs a big diamond' (87). The question is why does she need to get her own flowers if her man is an incurable romantic?

Meanwhile, the main focaliser in the chapter, Louise, appears to be incredibly sensitive, as she wonders 'what poor bugger had dug' her diamond 'out of the heart of darkness' (88). This is, of course, a discreet reference to Joseph Conrad's novel of the same name. This suggests that she is a book-reader, making her appear even more sympathetic to the reader.

'A' Level Revision Notes – When Will There Be Good News

She does not like doctors, although Joanna Hunter may be 'the exception to the rule', yet her love interest, Patrick, is 'an orthopaedic surgeon' (88). This makes Louise appear hypocritical.

We discover she works for the police and met Patrick at the scene of an horrific car accident on the M8. She realises that romantic meeting is full of contradictions: 'bloodthirsty yet faint-hearted' (89).

She worries about her son, Archie, driving, after what she has seen as 'chief inspector' (89). Patrick seems more accepting than Louise, as his philosophy is 'Life's random' (90).

Louise relinquishes 'control' and allows Patrick to take over her life in an 'authoritative' but 'amiable' way when they marry (91). He seems to be 'taming' her (91).

The narrative switches to Patrick's perspective, as we discover his late wife, Samantha, died in a car crash. It shows, once again, he accepts the quirks of fate, although he regrets that 'he hadn't been able to fix her' (92).

'A' Level Revision Notes – When Will There Be Good News

We find out that Patrick is 'relaxed about everything', although he did insist that Louise's son, Archie, attended their wedding (93). Strangely, he allowed his own son, Jamie, 'a real boy' unlike 'her little Pinocchio', to miss the occasion (93). Perhaps, he's as hypocritical as Louise.

Nautical imagery comes to the fore once more, as the narrative switches back to Louise's perspective. We discover she's had psychological 'therapy' and 'put all her negative thoughts' in 'a chest at the bottom of the sea' (94). At that point, Louise realises 'nothing else' is left after her negative thoughts are dispensed with (95). Jenny, the therapist, appears to agree that Louise lacks 'positive thoughts' (95). We feel sympathy for Louise, although she appears to be dangerously troubled.

Nevertheless, despite all her personal problems, Louise manages to get Archie in line by putting him into a private school where he becomes a 'geek' (96). Meanwhile, she considers how she could show off her 'MA in literature' with an imaginary daughter, with whom she could 'chat about the Brontes and George Eliot' (96).

She seems proud of her ability to 'shoot something and

'A' Level Revision Notes – When Will There Be Good News

skin it and eat it' (97). She is being portrayed as a formidable woman. She is almost a female version of Sherlock Holmes in that she is a little detached and almost superhuman.

Louise considers how running 'fast' kept Joanna Hunter alive, while Alison Needler 'hid' (98). We wonder who Alison is and what significance she has to the plot. We discover that Archie has 'elected to board' at school rather than 'live' with his mother (98). This again, shows us how Louise is distant and struggles to develop strong, trusting relationships.

She has a lot on her mind: violent memories of previous cases. We discover that Louise met 'Alison Needler, six months before the murders, although we don't find out the details, arousing the reader's curiosity (99).

Another character is revealed, as we meet Marcus McLellen, a rugby player 'baby DC', whom Louise has supported, 'shouting herself hoarse' in the process (99, 100). We find out that Marcus is investigating the unexpected burning of an 'amusement arcade owned by none other than lovely Dr Joanna Hunter's husband, Neil' (101). It reminds us of Neil's 'sticky patch', earlier in the novel. Could Neil have resorted to crime to get

'A' Level Revision Notes – When Will There Be Good News

insurance money? It is another question in the reader's mind. Marcus reveals that although Neil has been involved in two previous businesses that were razed to the ground, he is still considered 'a legitimate businessman' (102).

Louise follows up the investigation, 'pretending to be the kind of woman who was interested in romantic anecdotes', so she can find out how Joanna met Neil. Her fascination with Joanna, may have something to do with her reading through Neil's 'father-in-law's canon', although it's difficult to see how she sustains that interest. However, it serves as another mystery for the reader to unravel.

Louise's obsessive nature is clearly revealed, as we hear her 'superintendent' has suggested she should 'move on a little' from her absorption in the Needler case (105).

Suspense and tension increases significantly when we discover that the murderer of Joanna Hunter nee Mason's family is 'Andrew Decker', is 'getting out' of prison (106, 107).

The chapter ends on a cliff-hanger, as Louise senses

'A' Level Revision Notes – When Will There Be Good News

danger will interrupt her plans to dine on 'sea bass', but answers her phone anyway. We wonder who it is and what that person wants.

'A' Level Revision Notes – When Will There Be Good News
Chapter 5: Sanctuary

We quickly get the feeling that Doctor Hunter is loved, by both her dog, Sadie, whose 'excitement' at her arrival is tangible, and her baby son, who prepares to 'catapult himself into the air' (108). The themes of love and danger are interlinked.

Joanna's warmth seems to remind Reggie of her own mother, who had also been affectionate 'before Gary, and before the Man-Who-Came-Before-Gary' (109).

Jo invites Reggie to join her at 'Jenners with Sheila', forgetting that she has to go to her 'friend's' (110). This comment makes Jo appear a little self-absorbed, as Reggie reminds her that 'Ms MacDonald isn't really' a friend (100).

Reggie tries to remember when she last saw her late mother, just before her fateful holiday. We can guess the mother must have drowned as Reggie recalls 'the embarrassingly revealing swimming costume in a horrible orange lycra that would turn out to be the last outfit she ever wore' (101). The French words: 'je reviens' appear again, which makes us think that in some way Reggie's mother will return from the dead or make her presence felt later in the novel.

'A' Level Revision Notes – When Will There Be Good News

Later, Reggie is ambushed by a criminal, almost like Pip is by Magwitch at the start of 'Great Expectations', which is the novel she is reading at 'the bus stop' (112).

'A' Level Revision Notes – When Will There Be Good News

Chapter 6: To Brig O' Dread Thou Com'st At Last

The narrative returns to Jackson, who is on an 'over-subscribed cattle truck of a train' (117). We feel some sympathy for his plight, as he reminisces about his previous life, as he observes 'a couple of burned-out squaddies' (117).

We discover that he was left money, so only works 'for Bernie' as 'a man couldn't lie idle' (118). While we can't fault Jackson's work ethic, we do wonder who Bernie is. We wonder if Bernie is a criminal, as we find out that it 'might not be a righteous cause' (118).

Julia claims that he is 'like Midas' and like the Greek mythological king, Jackson may be lucky with money, but seems to be suffering in other respects.
Opposite Jackson on the train is 'a fortyish blonde, buxom as an overstuffed turkey' and 'wearing siren-red lipstick' (120). The detailed description plus the reference to Greek mythology, through the word 'siren', seems to suggest that her story will become intertwined with Jackson's in some way. Jackson's charitable nature is emphasised as he offers his 'North Face jacket' to an 'old woman', who smiles and shakes her head in response (120). Once again, we warm to Jackson.

'A' Level Revision Notes – When Will There Be Good News

We discover that Jackson is a thinker and opinionated on the subject of love, which he sees as 'visceral', 'overpowering' and ferocious' amongst other things (121). It seems he has a negative view of love.

His bitterness towards love has come about because Julia claims the baby is not his, and he's even had to put up with the threats of the baby's father, 'Mr Arty-Farty photographer' (122). The alliterative nickname emphasises how angry Jackson is with the father of this 'unholy family' (122).

Julia and Jonathan Carr are described as 'soft southerners', who live 'in his homeland, his heartland' (123). Jackson's resentment is almost tangible.
We hear about his 'murdered' sister, Niamh, and we wonder who he is texting the words: 'Miss you' (124). Our sympathy and curiously increase in equal measure. We find out that he thinking about Louise, who still sends him 'the occasional text' when she is 'drunk' (125). We feel his loneliness, isolation and disappointment that she got 'married' (125).

He thinks of Julia, 'playing Helen in "Doctor Faustus" in a stripped-down production' as he lustfully imagines going into the toilet with 'the woman in red' (126).

'A' Level Revision Notes – When Will There Be Good News

Despite his lack of romance in this imagined encounter, we sympathise with him somewhat as, unlike Julia, 'he had never been what you would call promiscuous' (127). Nevertheless, we wonder if we can trust this third person narrative that tells the story from Jackson's perspective.

Julia seems callous, especially in comparison with Jackson, as she mentions that his sister, Amelia, who is suffering from cancer, will be having her breasts 'lopped off' (127). Although, Julia also says: 'Poor Milly', we sense she doesn't really care from her previously insensitively graphic description (127).

By contrast, Jackson's sensitivity is highlighted when he isn't sure how to tell 'the old woman' that she can't see 'the Angel of the North' in the dark (128). He breaks the news to her 'gently', which makes him appear sympathetically to the reader (128).

He clearly doesn't know where he's going, as he's accidentally boarded a train for Edinburgh. His attitude towards the 'woman in red' with her 'ample and healthy breasts' makes him seem like a man who regards women as sexual objects (129). This will not endear him to many readers, although some may consider it an understandable human foible that makes him a more rounded character.

Once again, Greek mythology comes to the fore as we discover that Julia believes 'in the Fates' (130). Her superstition makes her appear to be strange. In comparison, Jackson appears to be relatively normal.

Jackson asks Julie 'innocently' whether the Fates are 'the same thing as the Furies' and he receives the enigmatic response: 'Don't even go there' (131). She seems so negative, so the reader is unlikely to warm to her.

'A' Level Revision Notes – When Will There Be Good News

Chapter 7: Satis house

This chapter is named after Miss Havisham's house in 'Great Expectations'. We expect to meet an old bitter spinster, like the character in the Charles Dickens novel. We are not disappointed, when Ms Macdonald opens the door at her 'bleak bungalow in Musselburgh' (132). Like Miss Havisham, Ms Macdonald is fragile as we discover that 'her left eye is bloodshot as if a red star had exploded in her brain' (132).

Like Miss Havisham, Ms Macdonald watches Reggie 'with a kind of vicarious thrill', which is similar to the relationship the Dickens character has with her protégé, Estella (133).

Cynicism about religion is evident, as we hear that Ms MacDonald is 'a pretribulationist', which means she will be 'whizzed up to heaven, business class' when she dies (134). Highlighting her extremism, Ms MacDonald thinks Reggie is 'going to hell', as she's not been 'saved' by religion (135, 134). Ms MacDonald's affection for her dog, Banjo, is likened to Hitler being 'very fond of his dog' (135). The exaggerated comparison makes Reggie, the focaliser, appear to be a typical teenager.

Reggie feels strangely comforted by 'Ms MacDonald's

'A' Level Revision Notes – When Will There Be Good News

flock of loony-tunes' praying for her and feeling sorry for her, 'on account of her orphan status' (136). We are subtly reminded that she is like Pip from 'Great Expectations' in this respect. Meanwhile, she can't bear the thought of Dr Hunter seeing her in this light, as she wants to be seen as 'heroically, cheerfully competent' (136). She is being portrayed as a plucky heroine.

Like Miss Havisham's house, Ms MacDonald's home is in a state of disrepair, which reflects how near she is to death. Ms MacDonald's house is filthy, as 'no one seemed to have told' her 'that cleanliness is next to godliness' (137). We can't help but think the worst of Ms MacDonald, while feeling sorry for Reggie, who does 'the washing up' and cleans 'the worst bits of the kitchen' like a Cinderella-type character (137).

Reggie considers how she'd opt to worship Diana, also known as 'Artemis, pale moon goddess of the chase and chastity' if she had to choose a religion (138). This shows that Reggie deeply considers everything and feels disillusioned with the opposite sex, which explains why she can relate to a 'powerful virgin' goddess (138).

Reggie's cynicism seems borne from the fact that her mother has had some awful experiences with the

'A' Level Revision Notes – When Will There Be Good News

opposite sex, including Gary, who 'courted' her 'with cheap hothouse roses from the Shell Shop' (139) Before her untimely death, her mother gratefully received anything that comes her way, including a presumably cheap holiday with Gary in 'Lloret de Mar'. Her mother's lack of culture is highlighted by the contrast with Reggie, who is translating the 'Iliad' and even knows that 'Sangria' comes from the same Latin root as 'blood' (141). Ironically, it seems, Reggie's mother was drinking 'a lot of Sangria' shortly before her death (141).

Reggie notices that some of Ms MacDonald's books are missing, like 'the second volume of the Iliad, the first of the Aenid' (142). The reader wonders about the significance of this. This narrative technique is used to arouse the reader's curiosity and is typically found in the detective genre.

Meanwhile, we discover that Reggie's mother died in Spain, when 'her beautiful long hair' became 'trapped in a drain' in the swimming pool (143). This makes all the nautical imagery that has preceded this revelation appear to make more sense. We wonder if another character will be drowned or die a watery death. It seems an unlikely way to die, so the reader expects that skullduggery was involved in Reggie's mother's death.

'A' Level Revision Notes – When Will There Be Good News

Reggie's sensitivity is clear when she wishes she could have her 'Mum's hair as a momento' (144). Again, this makes her appealing to the reader, especially in comparison to Gary, who only turns 'philosophical after the third Carlsberg' (144). He appears again in the very supermarket where her mother used to work 'in the company of a woman with too much henna in her hair' (145). Once again, he appears to be completely insensitive.

Meanwhile, Banjo, Ms MacDonald's dog, is portrayed as pitifully light, as Reggie observes 'how little he' weighs 'compared to the baby' (146). Despite all her religion, Ms MacDonald is guilty of animal cruelty through neglect. It implies she is hypocritical or that her religion involves tough love.

Finally, the narrative becomes more gothic in tone, as Reggie imagines Cathy coming 'home to Wuthering Heights' or her mother's 'ghost looking for' her (147).

'A' Level Revision Notes – When Will There Be Good News
Chapter 8: Rapture Ready

The alliterative title seems to foreshadow the death of Ms MacDonald, who has already made it sound as if she is prepared for the afterlife, given that she expects to go to heaven.

Somewhat surprisingly, we see the ensuing action from the point of view of Jackson. We wonder how the narrative strands will intertwine.

Although Jackson is 'checking the drunk guy's vital signs' after his collapse on the train, he is also looking at the woman in red's 'ferocious spiked heels (148). This makes him appear a victim of female ferocity, especially as we hear the story of when he was attacked at a hen night by a woman wearing similar shoes.

The 'smell of burning' accompanied by 'a high-pitch shrieking noise' precedes the carriage tipping 'to one side', as Jackson appears to be a victim of a train crash. Once again, Jackson is portrayed as unlucky character.

Finally, when everything stops moving, he wonders 'if everyone else' is 'dead' (150). People start to 'cry out' (150). It appears that Jackson is destined to live a life of suffering, so we have an increasing amount of sympathy for him, although we suspect he is something of a womaniser.

However, his survival instincts kick in and he quickly realises that they need to evacuate 'in double-quick time' (151). This shows how decisive he can be.
He tries to help a man, but this attempt is more like 'Butch and Sundance going over the cliff' (152). This analogy portrays Jackson as a romantic hero, like either of the aforementioned cowboys.

The narrative slowly reveals that Jackson knows what has 'happened now', but the reader has to wait for clarity, which creates more suspense (153). He is lying in a 'kind of gully' with 'one of the squaddies', which makes him think 'of his grandfather's brother going over the top at the Somme' (154). Heroism seems to run in the family.

Jackson is quoting 'himself to death' with lines from 'Doctor Faustus' (155). Perhaps he, like Faustus, has courted ill-fortune with hubris, or excessive pride. Nevertheless, Jackson's love of literature suggests a certain sensitivity. He tries to focus on his daughter, Marlee's face, so it will be 'the last thing' he sees before

'A' Level Revision Notes – When Will There Be Good News

he goes 'into the black tunnel', which is a euphemism for death.

'A' Level Revision Notes – When Will There Be Good News

Chapter 9: The Discreet Charm of the Bourgeoisie

The title references Marxist ideology and seems to suggest that the reader will feel some sympathy for the middle class.

Louise is the narrative focus and once again the phrase, used in an earlier chapter: 'she should have got the flowers' repeats (157). As readers, we are left to puzzle what it actually means and whether or not it is significant.

We hear that Alison Needler's life is 'a train wreck', the metaphor linking to Jackson's predicament (158). We wonder again whether he is alive, which extends the effect of the cliff-hanger ending in the previous chapter. We just as sorry for Joanna as we do for Alison, as the doctor is likely to be chased by 'the press', as well having to deal with the news that the killer of her family has been released (159). We discover that like Louise, Joanna lives in an 'unrelenting middle-class ghetto', an oxymoron which here indicates that they live where there is a distinct lack of night-time entertainment (159). Patrick tells Louise to 'rejoice in good fortune', now that she lives in quiet, seemingly safe area (160). We get the

'A' Level Revision Notes – When Will There Be Good News

feeling that the area won't be safe now that Decker is on the loose, which adds tension to the narrative.

David Needler's attack on Alison's family acts as a grim reminder about what Decker did to Joanna: 'three lives, three deaths' (161). The short sentences emphasise how lives were cut and snuffed out prematurely. Louise thinks of the reality that faces women: only 'somewhere, in some Utopian somewhere' can women walk 'without fear' (162). We feel greater sympathy for all the female characters in the novel, at this point. Meanwhile, Louise, rightly or wrongly, believes 'that nurturing' isn't 'in her mitochondrial DNA' (163). She thinks this because she thinks she is 'generic all incapable of growing things' (163). However, she seems quite obsessed with flowers and maybe is lacking confidence only, which makes the reader feel sympathetically towards her. Even the narrative reveals that Louise is not 'so blunt-headed' that she can't appreciate 'the love of a good man' (164).

As Louise remembers Joanna's father's 'several' wives, she thinks of the Robert Browning poem, 'My Last Duchess' (165). This does not paint Howard Mason in an attractive light; it almost implies he might have had something to do with Joanna's mother's murder.

'A' Level Revision Notes – When Will There Be Good News

Louise thinks of the killer, Andrew Decker, and how he 'surprise, surprise' had been a 'model prisoner' before his early release (166). She wishes that prisons were more like they used to be. The reader can feel that Louise simply feels protective towards Joanna, which casts her in a positive light.

Louise thinks that Decker may 'have another twenty years left in him' and is cynical about his 'degree in philosophy' (167). Does it really suggest that he is a reformed character? We wonder the same thing. Louise's thoughts switch back to Alison, who she thinks should 'get a big dog', which might offer some protection (168).

Once again we hear 'she should have got the flowers', which will make 'it look as if she' cares (169). She admits she does care, but 'possibly not quite enough' (169). However, we cannot necessary trust her opinion. The narration appears to be unreliable in that it is too harsh on her. She's going to be late home, so she apologises.

Alison appears at the window with 'cigarette smoke curling around her head like an aura' (170). She seems

'A' Level Revision Notes – When Will There Be Good News

to be a working-class angel, a former 'part-time admin assistant at Napier' (170). Her portrayal is not as sympathetic as Joanna's, although she is also an innocent victim.

Louise considers herself a 'bad wife' for thinking of Jackson Brodie, but she certainly is a good policewoman, working overtime to protect Alison (171). Once again, she is too harsh on herself.
She worries if she 'would look boorish if she [...] got a beer from the fridge' upon arriving at her house (172). Once again, she exhibits more sensitivity than she acknowledges to herself.

'The Last Duchess' reference appears again, as Louise considers how 'the first Mrs de Winter' lingers on 'in her belongings', like the 'Wedgewood' plates they eat off (173). Once again, Louise appears to be oversensitive. She thinks of a poem called 'The Mistletoe Bride', about a bride who hid and subsequently suffocated (174). The theme of death by asphyxiation is repeated here.

Louise seems more at home at work. Here in her house, she admits she has temporarily lost 'her own inner adult' (175). Perhaps she cannot function socially.
She has a 'knee-jerk reaction to the accent of the

dominant culture', as she struggles to deal socially with her in-laws (176).

She is full of negative thoughts, some of which are understandable, as we discover her diamond ring was bought 'with some of the money invested from Samantha's life insurance' (177). She seems haunted by Patrick's dead wife, but suspect paranoia.

Louise's mind flits back to Jackson, and their 'chaste' relationship which is likened to 'protagonists in an Austen novel' (178). It makes Jackson appear to be a romantic hero again. The connection between them appears stronger than she realises, as when she looks in the mirror, she thinks she looks like 'someone who had been in a terrible accident' (179). It foreshadows the news conveyed by Patrick, that there's 'been a train crash' (180).

'A' Level Revision Notes – When Will There Be Good News
Chapter 10: The Celestial City

The narrative switches to Jackson's perspective, as he sees himself in a cliched heaven, which is more like a 'very brightly lit' corridor than a tunnel (183).

He returns to 'the Land of Pain', as someone punches him 'in the chest' (184). He wonders who is stopping him 'going with his sister', who is 'beckoning' him (185).

Another short chapter increases the pace of the narrative, making events seem a blur like they are for the characters involved.

'A' Level Revision Notes – When Will There Be Good News

Part III: Tomorrow

Chapter 11: The Dogs They Left Behind

This first chapter of Part 3: Tomorrow sounds as if it will be about the past, suggesting that no matter what we do in the future we will be haunted by what has already happened to us. We've already had Part 1: In The Past and Part 2: Today, so at the very least it shows the passage of time.

We wonder how much time as passed as we return to Reggie's perspective. She's talking to Mr Hunter who explains that Joanna's aunt has 'only just been taken ill' (189). Reggie feels like she's 'a nuisance' to Mr Hunter, as he tells her 'impatiently' on the phone 'at an unearthly time' (189). It raises the tension as we can't help but not believe this excuse, especially as Reggie replies: 'She's never mentioned an aunt' (189).

Reggie can't believe it either, as it is so out of character for Dr Hunter not to call her herself as she 'always had her mobile with her' (190).

She's told 'it'll be nice' for her to 'have some time off', but it's the last thing she wants (191). Mr Hunter

48

'A' Level Revision Notes – When Will There Be Good News

appears as insensitive as her aunt Linda, who simply dismissively tells Reggie after the loss of her mother: 'Well, take care of yourself then, Regina' (191).

She longs to tell Dr Hunter about the events of the train crash, but now will have to wait. She considers Mr Hunter 'an unsatisfactory audience at the best of times', so once again via contrast, he is portrayed unsympathetically.

The GMTV news reporter reveals the details: 'Fifteen people dead, four critical, many severely injured' from which we can assume that Jackson is still near to death (193).

We find out Reggie was 'too upset to comment' after her mother's death, yet the media intruded on her privacy anyway (194). We expect the same is happening again, as the media are portrayed as heartless and making a living out of other people's 'tragedies' (194).

Reggie, by contrast, is extremely sentimental, refusing to part with her mother's possessions and taking 'over the occupation of' her bedroom (195).

'A' Level Revision Notes – When Will There Be Good News

She's even upset over Ms MacDonald demise and the fact that 'she had had her last supper' (196). We discover that the old lady has caused the crash, by knocking down a bridge in her car and falling onto the train 'track below' (196).

Reggie, meanwhile, must have behaved heroically in the aftermath of the crash, as she is told by a paramedic: 'You gave him a chance' (197). We can safely assume that it's Jackson who has been whisked away 'in a helicopter' (197).

She is self-conscious about her appearance in 'Ms MacDonald's grotty dressing gown' and her attraction to 'the Asian guy' suggests that she is not going to be the old maid she predicts she will be when she grows older (198). It reminds us that we can't believe everything we are told in the narrative.

Nevertheless, Reggie tries to think logically, mentioning that Ms MacDonald's crash might have been because of her 'brain tumour' (199).

Reggie was told she will have identify the body

'A' Level Revision Notes – When Will There Be Good News

'tomorrow' and now that day is here (200). We are made to feel more sorry for her, as she is almost saintly, visiting her 'Mum's grave every week' (201).

Now that Banjo, the dog, has also died, she closes 'his dim eyes' (202). She feels 'cursed' (202). We can imagine her as 'an usherette' in a cinema, like a mother, shining her torch on death in the darkness after the train crash (202). Dealing with death has almost become like a dirty job for her.

She resuscitates Jackson, despite all the difficulties, 'like a large awkward spider' (203). This is strange simile, as it would normally indicate prey and death. However, in this case it suggests that Reggie desperately clings onto life and never gives up, like the spider in the Robert the Bruce tale.

Another mention of 'the Somme' suggests that, metaphorically speaking, Reggie has been through the wars (204). She is now suffering the embarrassment of being laughed at on the bus, wearing the clothes 'of a middle-aged, born-again ex-teacher' (205).

Reggie recalls the 'postcard with a picture of Bruges' that she pulled out of Jackson's jacket from Marlee

'A' Level Revision Notes – When Will There Be Good News (206). She remembers her mother's postcard from Spain, which was also 'touched with death' (207). She certainly does appear to be cursed.

'A' Level Revision Notes – When Will There Be Good News

Chapter 12: Adam Lay Ybounden

The chapter is named after a fifteenth-century English text about the fall of mankind, amongst other things, so it implies that what follows maybe about something similar.

It quickly becomes apparent that we are viewing events from Jackson's perspective as he reveals he is 'not dead then' (208). He feels like he is inhabiting some ghastly 'halfway house' between life and death (208).

Dead relations and acquaintances visit him, but they are 'vague round the edges' (209). He finds the experience so 'exhausting' that he eventually wakes up to a 'fuzzy' nurse (210). It appears there is no solace in life or death for Jackson.

'A' Level Revision Notes – When Will There Be Good News
Chapter 13: Outlaw

Louise's in-laws appear to be complete unaffected by the train crash, as Bridget and Tim sleep 'undisturbed' (211). Meanwhile, Louise feels 'drained' from the experience, while Patrick remains his usual 'chipper self', despite all his hard work (211). The contrast makes the latter pair appear almost too good to be true. Louise doesn't ask Bridget what she does in her spare time as she fears the answer will 'irritate' her (212). Meanwhile, Tim is portrayed as 'holding a hand to his forehead effetely', as he decides he doesn't want to know about the 'food miles' of the 'Mexican raspberries' (212).

Once again, we, as readers are meant to feel sorry for Louise, who 'never had a father to speak of' and a mother who was forever 'puking her guts up like the best of badly behaved teenagers' (213, 212).

Patrick acts fatherly towards Louise, despite her rude outburst towards his family, reminding her that she 'should eat', despite the trials and tribulations of that night (214). He remains patient with her, touching her 'gently, as if she were sick' (215). He invites her to 'Glamis' with them for golf, but she turns him down

'A' Level Revision Notes – When Will There Be Good News

(216). Obviously, the place has Macbeth and therefore bloodshed and disloyalty connotations.

Louise calls in on Neil Hunter, who is described as 'a wolf in wolf's clothing' (217). Although he is far from ugly physically, he is portrayed as everything that Joanna isn't, smelling of 'last night's whisky' (217).

She begins questioning him about his wife's whereabouts and he seems 'nervous' (218). He appears to have 'liar' written all 'through him, like a stick of rock' (219). Once again, we hear Joanna is in Hawes, which is pronounced 'whores' for comic effect (220).

Neil calls Louise 'doll', which makes him appear sexist (221). She calls him 'doll' in return, when he looks worried about a sudden phone call, so his sexist words backfire. Once again, the main protagonist gets the upper hand.

While Neil is out on the phone, Louise looks at Joanna's noticeboard, which seems to tells the world that she is 'no longer the victim' (222). We are meant to admire Joanna as much as we loathe Neil.

'A' Level Revision Notes – When Will There Be Good News

When he returns to the room, he makes an attempt at 'bonhomie' with Louise, which is read as 'false' (223). Neil appears to be a villain, or the 'outlaw' in the title of the chapter.

'A' Level Revision Notes – When Will There Be Good News
Chapter 14: The Famous Reggie

This chapter appears to indicate that Reggie will become a media heroine for what she has done by saving Jackson's life.

We hear about the casual racism directed towards Mr Hussain, who runs the local corner shop before Reggie returns to what is troubling her: the 'hesitation' of Mr Hunter before he revealed to her that Joanna's aunt is named 'Agnes' (224). We can't help but think he is a poor liar and that Reggie could rival Louise with her powers of detection.

We feel sorry for Reggie again as relives how she was 'sick' after eating 'pancakes' after her mother's death (225).

She lives in a 'close' that 'always' smells unpleasant, so you get the feeling she is trapped (226). Her tenement is described as near 'an abandoned bonded warehouse' with 'black-barred windows as grim as anything in Dickens' (226-7). We can imagine that this will be the scene of a future crime rather than 'a new Tesco Metro' (227).

'A' Level Revision Notes – When Will There Be Good News

In fact, the most threatening thing about her living quarters is the note stuck on her front 'door with chewing gum'. It reads: 'Reggie Chase - you cant hide from us' (228). We wonder who could want to hurt such an innocent girl. The lack of punctuation in the note implies a lack of education and therefore mercy. It makes it all the more threatening.

Once she discovered that her home has been ransacked, she gives out 'a little cry' (229). Once again, we sympathise with this innocent victim.

The pace of the narrative quickens, as she is sent 'sprawling into the shower' by a 'hefty shove' (230, 229). She fears the two male assailants may 'kill' or 'rape' her (230).

She escapes that fate, but one of them tosses her a copy of the 'Iliad' to her 'like a grenade' (231). She thinks of 'Trojan horses', which links to how she seems to have been betrayed by her brother, Billy, even though these 'idiots' have come 'looking for a guy called "Reggie"' (231).

'A' Level Revision Notes – When Will There Be Good News

She wishes she has a big dog like Sadie, so people would think 'twice about messing with you' (232). That thought emphasises how vulnerable and defenceless she is.

Reggie returns to the mystery of Doctor Hunter's disappearance. Usually, Sadie goes everywhere with the doctor, but she distinctly hears her 'bark in the background' when on the phone to Mr Hunter (233). Once again, the reader suspects skullduggery.

'A' Level Revision Notes – When Will There Be Good News
Chapter 15: Missing in Action

The title links to Jackson's time in the army, which is relevant given that metaphorically he's in the wars. His practical side, tattooing his blood type: 'A Positive' above his heart may have just saved him from certain death (234).

Jackson feels suspicious of the doctors, but he is not in good shape, unsurprisingly, as virtually all he can say is 'fuzzy' (235).

A nurse tells him he is 'Andrew Decker', as that's who he is, according to the 'wallet' in his jacket pocket (236). We wonder what will happen to him, as he is too weak and too confused to argue.

We hear he is 'a clock without hands' and 'a blank sheet of paper' (237). Like Reggie, he is extremely vulnerable. We find out he has been in hospital for 'twenty hours' and since he has lost his memory; he clearly believes that he is Decker (238).

'A' Level Revision Notes – When Will There Be Good News
Chapter 16: Reggie Chase, Girl Detective

Reggie has already shown signs of being a budding detective and this title confirms it. She turns up at the Hunters, noticing minute details, like 'a smear of lipstick on the rim' of an empty mug on the table (239). It is 'pale coral, not Dr Hunter's colour' (239). Once again, Neil appears to be an evil, cheating husband, who is not good enough for Joanna.

He tries to change the subject to Reggie's appearance, which he says is 'worse' than he feels (240).

Like a dogged detective, Reggie is not put off. She asks for Aunt Agnes's 'phone number' (241). Unsurprisingly, Mr Hunter refuses to give it to her, on account of Agnes needing 'peace and quiet' (241). His excuses are unconvincing.

The scene soon changes to the hospital as we find out that Ms MacDonald doesn't look 'as bad as Reggie expected' when she peers at the corpse (242). This shows how mature she is.

Switching back to the original scene, her doggedness pays off, as Mr Hunter finally allows her to drop her

'A' Level Revision Notes – When Will There Be Good News

'Topshop bag' there (243). It's a small victory, but it shows she knows the benefits of never giving up.

Mr Hunter only gives Reggie 'half' the money she is owed and we find out Joanna is scared he'll go 'ballistic' if he finds out about 'the spare car keys that she' keeps on 'a shelf in the garage' (244). This makes him sound even less sympathetic to the reader.

Another mystery is added to the narrative, as we find out that 'Dr Hunter's Toyota Prius' is still in the garage (245). Her husband claimed that she 'drove' to her aunt's, so clearly he lied (245).

Mr Hunter wants her to look after the dog and, true to form, has not mentioned 'money for dog food' (246). This shows how mean he is.

Now that he is gone, Reggie can pry behind the scenes at the Hunter's. There she discovers that Joanna has left wearing her work suit, which is 'completely out of character' (247).

The pace quickens as Mr Hunter suddenly returns and Reggie has to pretend she has 'just been to the loo' (248). Apart from hearing Dr Hunter's ring tone she now

'A' Level Revision Notes – When Will There Be Good News

has another clue, thanks to Sadie: the baby's bloodstained 'moss-green blanket' (249).

Like a beast of burden, Reggie's mother used to tell her she was 'bred from a donkey', a description that evokes more sympathy (250).

In Dr Hunter's surgery, Reggie again shows her detective skills as she develops a line of questioning with the 'starchy' receptionist (251). Reggie is not one to be put off the scent easily.

As she flees from the hostile receptionist, she bumps into Sheila, 'one of the midwives' (252). Another unexplained event is revealed, as Sheila tells Reggie that not turning up 'to Jenners last night' is 'not Jo' (253).

Reggie bravely pretends everything is 'OK', and before the close of the chapter thinks of how 'a pocket' is 'where prostitutes' keep 'their money', according to the mercenary-sounding Mr Hunter (254).

'A' Level Revision Notes – When Will There Be Good News
Chapter 17: Pilgrim's Progress

The narrative switches back to Jackson, and we wonder how this chapter will work as an allegory like the book it is named after. Does it mean that the trials and tribulations endured by the protagonist are symbolic of something else?

Jackson wakes up after a nightmare involving the woman from the Dales, albeit one with 'no face' (255). At least, he remembers his name now.

He can't work out why he is in Edinburgh though, as he was on his 'way to London' (256). We wonder why he thinks Tessa might have 'joined him' (256).

'A' Level Revision Notes – When Will There Be Good News
Chapter 18: Nada y Pues Nada

The reference to Ernest Hemingway's short story appears again and we can imagine it may be about death, as the word 'nothing' ('nada') appears twice. Reggie returns to Ms MacDonald's house and lies to the police. She justifies it with the words: 'One lie, one truth' (273). She believes they cancel each other out and leave 'the world unchanged' (273).

Reggie thinks of how Inspector Louise Monroe doesn't 'really look like a policewoman', partly because she wears 'the same off-duty clothes as Dr Hunter' (274). This makes Louise seem more sympathetic and ties her more directly to the original victim, Joanna.

We revisit Louise's words: 'I'm very tired' from Reggie's perspective, so that adds some veracity to the narrative (275).

Louise is 'sceptical' of Reggie's account of the night before's train crash, but we can accept that attitude is the result of her job (276).

As Reggie enters Ms MacDonald's house, the massive 'bone-white moon' emphasises how close she has been to death and makes us remember how her own life is under threat (277).

Reggie recalls a conversation with Dr Hunter, where she reveals that she wants 'to know when' she is 'going to die' (278). She thinks she can 'avoid a premature death at the hands of idiots' (278). This proves she is a fighter.

Before she sleeps, she thinks of more questions: 'why had Dr Hunter stepped out of her shoes and walked out of her life' (279). It reminds the reader of the unanswered mystery of Joanna's disappearance.

'A' Level Revision Notes – When Will There Be Good News
Chapter 19: Ad Lucem

The title translated means 'into the light', seemingly to indicate Jackson's recovery is gathering speed.
He is not allowed his phone though, as the nurse tells him he needs to 'rest' even 'if it kills' him (280).

He hears a 'familiar' voice and has 'a moment of supernatural clarity' (281). 'Her eyes' are 'black pools of exhaustion', which doesn't seem to augur well (282). However, he tells her he loves her. We may feel as confused as him, as readers.

'A' Level Revision Notes – When Will There Be Good News

Chapter 20: Fiat Lux

The translation of the chapter is 'let there be light', so once again it links to Genesis and appears to be more optimistic than events would seem to suggest. Louise's predicament of not being 'able to eat meat in days' does not augur well (283). Neither does her lack of comment to Alison, who asks: 'Don't you have a home to go to?' (284).

She has clearly been 'disorientated' by Jackson's 'declaration' that he loves her, although the 'spell' is broken by him 'asking for his wife' (285). Nevertheless, he does seem to have a magical connection with her: hence the word: 'spell'.

It throws into contrast her relationship with Patrick. The words 'my husband' are 'stones in her mouth' (286). She thinks she is the 'wrong woman' for the 'right man' and blames herself (285).

As she pours herself a red wine and relaxes, she enjoys the feeling, which 'is like being single again' (287).

Her mind flits to Joanna and she reassures herself that

'A' Level Revision Notes – When Will There Be Good News

there is 'nothing suspicious at all' about her disappearance (288). It seems that Reggie is the more perceptive detective.

When Patrick and her in-laws return home, she feigns sleep and reminds herself she was only a 'whisker' away from saying 'I love you too' to Jackson (289).

'A' Level Revision Notes – When Will There Be Good News
Chapter 21: Grave Danger

The title of this chapter is straightforward and centred on Joanna, who we have already guessed is not at her aunt's. Now it is being confirmed that she is in a lot of trouble.

She wakes 'in a strange bed' with Martina opening the curtains (290). We feel as disorientated and confused as she does as we see that the light streaming through is 'unusual, bright and alien' (290).

We are reminded that Martina is her father's ex and we wonder now if she is working with Neil somehow, as her 'cheerful upturned' smile seems to mean the opposite as we accept the contrast with Joanna's mother (291). We cannot trust Martina.

Joanna thinks of Decker's trial and how she was never her father's 'favourite' child (292). She feels like she should 'run', but she clutches her 'baby', who wakes with a 'squawk' (293).

The writer has effectively given us more questions than answers in this brief chapter.

'A' Level Revision Notes – When Will There Be Good News

Part IV: And Tomorrow

Chapter 22: Jackson Risen

It appears that Jackson is rising again like Jesus Christ, given the title. He has done so effectively from the dead, so it casts him in a somewhat holy light.

He recalls his dream and how he had 'let' Louise into 'his heart' (297). Interestingly, 'Tessa hadn't existed in his dream world' (298). We discover Tessa is his wife on the rebound, as 'he had proposed to her the day after Louise texted him to tell him she was getting married' (297).

He thinks about how 'the love of a good woman' turns 'you inside out and into another self you barely' recognise' (298). He appears to be reconsidering whether this relationship is right for him, a bit like Louise with Patrick.

His wife is just 'a vague, Tessa-shaped blur', and he tells the policewoman that he can't remember her, partly to stop her having to 'come back early from the States' (299).

'A' Level Revision Notes – When Will There Be Good News

He does reaffirm that he 'used to be a policeman', which seems to be the most important thing to say 'every time' he hits 'the dead end of the existential labyrinth' (300). He seems more married to his work than he is to Tessa. He briefly recalls his first wife, Josie, before thinking of his 'sins of omission' (301). By this, he means that he hasn't told Tessa about Nathan, his son. Jackson seems to have a guilty conscience.

He thinks of his curator wife trying to educate him on the subject of Assyria, but his brain being cluttered with 'useless old information' instead (302). This is ironic, as Assyria does not have any direct relevance to him and it is more ancient history than his own precious memories. He does not appear to be really living his life with Tessa; he is just going through the motions.

Josie calls his marriage to Tessa 'cradle-snatching', as she's only 'thirty-four' (303). He has been roundly condemned for marrying, even by Amelia, who had 'once been in love with Jackson' (303). His mind turns to Decker, as he wonders if he has his wallet. He feels as if he has been 'reborn naked', as he lacks his possessions (303).

'A' Level Revision Notes – When Will There Be Good News

He thinks of his sister, who was 'saving herself for Mr Right' (304). Instead, 'she was raped and murdered' (304).

Likewise, Tessa has had her fair share of heartache as her parents were 'killed in a car crash' (304). There is 'no sign they had ever existed', as Tessa says she likes to keep her 'life in the present' (305). She thinks, quoting Ruskin, 'that every increased possession loads us with weariness' (305).

Although he likes to think marriage suits him, Josie describes him as 'a lone wolf' and this is largely how he's been portrayed so far in the novel (306).

He thinks of how he met Tessa at Bernie's, when he finally said 'yes' to the invite to one of his 'famous soiriees' (307).

His practical side makes him different to those assembled there, as he thinks 'no woman should wear a pair of shoes that she couldn't, if necessary, run away in' (308).

'A' Level Revision Notes – When Will There Be Good News

Tessa describes him in nautical terms as 'a safe harbour' as she sidles up to him (309). Jackson is described as a 'lucky dog' by Bernie, who envies him for finding a girl 'fifteen years younger' (310).

Like his sister, Niamh, Tessa 'had been a convent girl' (311). You sense Tessa is part of his life to replace his sister.

Meanwhile, in the present, he is still 'a weak version of himself, a flawed clone' (312). Jackson considers the fact that his 'veins' run 'with the blood of strangers' after his operation (313).

Reggie, at his bedside, tells him that he belongs to her, as she 'saved' his life (314). Now he is in her 'thrall' and can only be released by 'reciprocation' (314). We expect that will happen. We wonder if Reggie really believes in 'Native American' folklore, but the chapter really serves to inform us that Jackson now really feels 'reborn' (315).

'A' Level Revision Notes – When Will There Be Good News
Chapter 23: Dr Foster Went to Gloucester

The nursery-rhyme sounding title concerns the doctor, who treated Jackson. We get the feeling that the plot will thicken.

The tone of the title refers to childish humour of 'the Famous Reggie', who says of Doctor Foster: 'He stepped in a puddle right up to his middle and never went that way again' (317).

Reggie is prepared to lie in order to stay with Jackson. 'I'm his daughter, Marlee', she says (318). Meanwhile, her generosity extends to her giving Jackson 'a ten-pound note' (319). We can't help but be impressed by her attitude. She assumes Jackson is 'an OK sort of person and we have no reason to believe she is incorrect (320).

While thinking of Jackson, she makes the word 'altruistic' her 'word of the day', but it applies to her more than him (321). We also discover that she 'was never going to be a person who didn't come back', so she means what she says when she tells Jackson she'll return, which is a recurring theme (322). She's worried that Dr Hunter won't return and it appears she'll ask Jackson to help, as 'detectives' know 'how to find people' (323)

'A' Level Revision Notes – When Will There Be Good News

Chapter 24: A Good Man Is Hard to Find

The narrative returns to Louise, who wakes up feeling 'a heavy weight' on her (324). Consequently, she is 'gasping for air' (324). We wonder if she has a guilty conscience for her treatment of the 'neat sleeper' she is lying next to (324). She still finds herself thinking of her 'chaste kiss for an invalid' with Jackson (325). She thinks of him in Arthurian terms, as 'the Fisher King, sick and emasculated' (326). He has almost legendary status for her.

She tries unsuccessfully to escape the house without talking to the in-laws, and has a quick exchange in which she says: 'No rest for the wicked', referring to herself (327). This indicates she is still suffering from a guilty conscience.

Like Reggie, she's the type that keeps her word and returns if she says she will. She informs Neil: 'I said I'd be back', when he's surprised at the unearthly time she's arrived at his doorstep (328).

He says Jo's 'aunt's phone number and address' is 'in the study', when Louise asks for it (329). It seems as if he's playing for time.

'A' Level Revision Notes – When Will There Be Good News

When Jo's phone rings in his absence, she answers it although she fears, by doing so, she is being 'intrusive' and 'unethical' (330). It shows she uses instinct to decide on the right course of action. It also gives the reader another unanswered question: who was the man on the other end of the line, who put the phone down. When Neil returns she improvises, saying she needs to see Dr Hunter's phone in case Decker has 'phoned' (331).

Neil hands over an address and number of 'Agnes Barker', who is 'like a character in a farce', such is her scepticism (332). Louise confiscates Jo's phone and can see 'no calls to and from Agnes' (333). Neil's story appears to be a lie to her, although the readers knew this some time before. She realises it is all 'smoke and mirrors' (334).

She watches Alison with her children, who are 'as docile as zombies' (335). This links them with death and emphasises how they are under threat. 'The winter solstice' indicates dark days are upon them (335). Louise goes to Sheila Hayes, feeling disturbed by the 'fecundity' all around her 'in the ante-natal clinic' (336). Louise appears to have a lot of hang-ups. Sheila

'A' Level Revision Notes – When Will There Be Good News

confirms that Jo's behaviour is 'very out of character' (337).

Abbie Nash helps Louise's investigation back at work, and she looks 'more imaginative than her badly cut hair' suggests (338). Louise is so upset that she cannot face eating and waves the offer of 'crisps away' (239). She has effectively discovered that Neil is lying when she starts Jo's Prius, leaving us with a cliffhanger as we wonder if she has enough evidence to make an arrest.

'A' Level Revision Notes – When Will There Be Good News
Chapter 25: Abide with Me

From the title, we can guess there will be aspects of loyalty and religion amongst the contents, as it refers to a hymn.

The narrative switches to Joanna, who remembers when 'Martina died' (340). This throws up more questions, as Jo had seen Martina in a previous chapter. Was it a dream?

She remembers how her father 'throws a 'bottle of whisky at her' when she conveys the news of Martina's note (341). Howard Mason continues to be portrayed as a monster.

Jo, also, cannot 'forgive her aunt for not wrapping her in love' in her father's absence (342). She is grateful that 'Howard put her into a boarding school that fostered her and cared for her', which made his death easier to deal with (343). We notice that she doesn't refer to him as 'Dad'.

She thinks about how 'safe' her child was when he was inside the womb (344). She considers that her 'whole life' is 'an act of bereavement' (345). It is as if none of it

'A' Level Revision Notes – When Will There Be Good News

is real. However, 'the bad man' is 'coming', so we are left on another cliffhanger (345). The use of the words 'bad man' make us think how traumatised she still is from the past.

'A' Level Revision Notes – When Will There Be Good News
Chapter 26: Reggie Chase, Warrior Virgin

Reggie appears to be the most dogged of all the detectives as she assumes correctly that Jo's phone has 'run out of battery' (346).

She also assumes as there is 'no Range Rover' outside the Hunters, then Neil must be out (347).

Inside she sees 'black' bananas and 'a large cobweb' (348). She thinks the place is turning to its 'primal state' (348). This scientific language links her to Dr Hunter. Two 'aggressive-sounding' cars approach, signalling that she must be careful, increasing the tension (349).

She sees a big man with a 'bull neck' and a 'bald head' saying: 'Time's running out, Neil' (350). We finally realise that Neil is being blackmailed. His wife and child have been 'kidnapped' (351). The pace quickens. Reggie heads off to speak to Louise and inform her of what she's found out, with 'the mysterious Aunt Agnes' address inside Jo's 'Filofax' (352).

When she gets home, she finds her place has been torched. We hear that 'Reggie's life' is 'like the Ilian plain, littered with dead', which links her to Homer's writings about the sacking of Troy again (353).

Mr Hussain picks up a piece of 'charred paper' floating in the air and reads it (354). Reggie recognises it as 'Ovid' (354). Perhaps it is to indicate that great poetry can come from tragic events.

She is confronted by 'Blondie and Ginger' again, seeing herself as 'the sister of the Artful Dodger', which links her to Dickens's 'Oliver Twist' titular character. The reader should feel more sympathy for her as a result.

She doesn't mean to cry but she is 'so tired' and upset, especially when hit in the face by 'the Aeneid' (356). Perhaps it indicates how closely connected all the narrative strands are, as the aforementioned novel is about a Trojan in Rome. The Iliad is about the Trojan War, so there are strong links between the two.

'A' Level Revision Notes – When Will There Be Good News

Chapter 27: Jackson Leaves The Building

This chapter could be seen as a self-conscious title on the part of the writer, who is only too aware of how long Jackson has been kept in the hospital in chapter after chapter, to make it seem that a lot has happened during the time he was on the mend.

Jackson is compared to 'Frankenstein's monster', on account of 'some metal staples in his forehead' (357). The fictional character he is being compared to has superhuman qualities and is sensitive, despite his gruesome appearance. The same could be said about Jackson now.

Jackson is desperate to get out and tries unsuccessfully to convince first Dr Foster and then 'the boy-wizard doctor' to let him go (358).

Reggie turns up with clothes bought at Topshop, so at least he has something to wear. Jackson wonders why she was given his old clothes and she admits lying: 'I said I was your daughter' (359). Reggie seems keen to become part of a family again, and now she has latched onto Jackson to fill a void in her life.

'A' Level Revision Notes – When Will There Be Good News

Reggie tries to convince Jackson to help her and 'save complete strangers' (360). These 'strangers' to Jackson are, of course, Dr Hunter and her baby. It's a cliffhanger of sorts, but we expect Jackson to accede to her demands.

'A' Level Revision Notes – When Will There Be Good News

Part V: And Tomorrow

Chapter 28: The Prodigal Wife

Now that a speech from the play 'Macbeth' is being quoted from near the time of his demise, we can't help but think 'the prodigal wife' may refer to a Lady Macbeth-type character. However, although Louise is strong enough for the comparison to work, she hasn't had a mental breakdown yet, so the similarity ends there.

Louis's partner on the drive to Hawes, Marcus, is 'handsome, polished and new' (365). We wonder if a love interest will develop, although she is 'old enough to be Marcus's mother' (365).

We hear about how Louise has lied to Patrick about her past, saying that she 'lost' her 'virginity at eighteen' (366). She seems to feel guilt as we hear 'she should have told the truth', especially about how she has 'no idea how to love another human being' (366).

She calls Patrick to say she'll be late and tries to start an argument. However, Patrick does not rise to the bait, telling her: 'You're your own worst enemy' (367). Of the two of them, he does appear to be the most loving and

'A' Level Revision Notes – When Will There Be Good News

therefore is the more sympathetic character to the reader.

She seems to want to get know Marcus better, and asks him why he wanted to 'join the police' (368). She guesses correctly that his clichéd answer will be: to 'make a difference' (368). However, she doesn't think any less of him, as a result, as he's the 'kind of boy any mother would like to have' (368). He even seems prepared to forgive Decker, to which Louise replies: 'What are you, Mother Teresa?' (369). Nevertheless, she realises that 'age' has made her 'hard and unfeeling' (369).

Louise thinks about how Patrick likes 'Restoration comedies', which is inn direct contrast to her taste for 'revenge tragedies' (370). The drive is geographically taking her away from him, while the distance is growing metaphorically too.

However, more positively, she is beginning to give credit to Reggie, whose 'fantasies were all proving to be grounded in reality' (371). Louise even utters the word to her partner that she has been 'avoiding': kidnap (372). She also avoids telling Marcus who the Nissan-

'A' Level Revision Notes – When Will There Be Good News

driver was 'who wasn't Decker' (373). It seems as if she is in denial.

She considers how she cannot 'figure herself into' Patrick's 'vision of the future', so it is difficult to see how their relationship can continue after this trip (374). Despite her lack of affinity for Hawes, where she now finds herself, she 'supposed she would go for Hawes' over Ireland, Patrick's homeland. (375).

She seems modest and generous though, as she says to Marcus: 'You can have the honours', after they discover the aunt's house is empty (376). It takes her efforts to uncover that the aunt is in 'a nursing home' though (377).

There's some dramatic irony as Louise is told by her colleagues that Decker has hired a Renault Espace 'with his daughter' (378). We, of course, know it's Jackson and Reggie, but even Louise knows Decker doesn't have a daughter, so she is not made to look stupid to the reader.

When they get to Fernlea, the nursing home, Louise asserts that she would rather 'lie down beneath a hedge' than 'come to a place like this' (379). It turns out that Agnes died 'a couple of weeks ago' (380). Louise is

'A' Level Revision Notes – When Will There Be Good News

so baffled that she admits to Marcus: 'I don't know who had anything to do with who any more' (381).

Louise lies to Marcus saying she feels 'fine', although she later falsely claims 'the time of the month' is making her behave strangely (382). She describes Reggie and Jackson as 'two of the most provoking people she could think of' and, after making a phone call, she realises that 'somehow' they are together (383). The theme of mistaken identity continues, as Lousie receives a call, telling her that Decker has been stopped 'on the A1' (384). Most importantly for the reader, we find out that Decker was visited by 'none other than one Dr Joanna Hunter', when he was in prison (385).

Meanwhile, Louise doesn't want to take any calls because 'it's always bad news', but she does anyway, only to find out that Jackson has been calling Joanna on her mobile, prior to her disappearance (386). Of course, it makes the reader think 'when will there be good news', echoing the title of the novel.

'A' Level Revision Notes – When Will There Be Good News
Chapter 29: Arma Virumque Cano

The chapter is named after the opening words of the 'Aeneid', which means: 'I sing of arms and of a man'. Unsurprisingly, the focus of our attention is Jackson, who fits the bill.

He is 'baffled' by the fact he is staying at Ms MacDonald's, the place where 'he had died and lived' again, after the train crash (387). He sees himself as 'like a tired old dog', which implies he's loyal, but lacks energy (388). He promises to pay Reggie back, as she's emptying her account to pay for expenses, and tells her he's 'rich' (389). Ironically, she doesn't believe it, although it's true.

His sensitive nature comes to the fore as we realise he couldn't board a train after the crash, as 'the climbing-back-on-the-horse theory' is 'all very well when' it is 'just a theory' (390). He feels traumatised and 'survivor guilt', as he thinks of those who lost their lives (391). He's not too proud to take on board good advice from Reggie, who tells him to 'breathe', to help rid himself of the 'heebie-jeebies' (392).

Meanwhile, he does still possess some mental toughness, shown when he bares 'his lone wolf teeth in

'A' Level Revision Notes – When Will There Be Good News

an attempt' to get a hire car, despite his lack of documentation (393).

In the end, it is the receptionist, Joy, being 'made redundant' that clinches the car hire deal (394). We get the feeling that Jackson enjoys his freedom, as he 'literally' only has 'the clothes he stood up in' (395). He's completely unlike Reggie, who is saddled with a lot. Perhaps it reflects each character's view of responsibility.

We wonder if Jackson will ever be the same again as he has 'a small, nagging doubt that he might not have been put back together in quite the same way as before' (396).

Jackson's impaired ability to drive results in a minor crash, which has the Espace 'facing the wrong way', a recurring theme for Jackson, who seems to have a penchant for making poor life decisions (397).

He finds himself 'brought down by two officers', which adds to the idea that he is riddled by bad luck (398). Reggie's dog-like loyalty is displayed when she fights Jackson's corner verbally against 'the army boys' like a

'A' Level Revision Notes – When Will There Be Good News

Jack Russell fending off a pack of Dobermans (399). He thinks of Louise, in his time of need, as 'she would do nicely' (400). Coincidentally she calls the phone in Reggie's backpack and he answers, saying 'that's amazing', when he realises who it is (401).

Unfortunately, the call is 'ended' by a policeman, which adds to the tension (401). Louise appears at the rescue, talking tough 'as if she was auditioning for "The Sweeney"' and taking charge (402).

'A' Level Revision Notes – When Will There Be Good News

Chapter 30: Road Trip

We can only guess that in this chapter there will be a lot more adventures on the way back to Scotland. Jackson tells Louise that he is 'not actually going in the same direction' as her, but for now he is in the same car with her, Reggie, Marcus and the dog (403).

Metaphorically and actually, Louise is in 'the driving seat' (404). She observes how 'tight the ring is on her finger', which implies she feels constrained by marriage (405). Once again, she is having second thoughts about her relationship with Patrick.

The subject returns to the business in hand: Jo's disappearance. Louise admits, like Reggie, she doesn't 'understand' what has happened, given the aunt has been dead for two weeks (406). It seems that Louise cannot think professionally for long when she's near Jackson, as now she soon interrogates him about what his wife is 'called ' (407).

Jackson, meanwhile, is still trying to fathom out what has happened to him. He lost 'his Blackberry in the train crash' and Louise asks: 'What else did you lose?' (408). Jackson reveals that he's also lost his 'credit cards, driving licence' and 'keys', as well as 'an address book

'A' Level Revision Notes – When Will There Be Good News

in the BlackBerry' (409). Louise tells him that Decker must have called Joanna Hunter using Jackson's phone, but he, like Reggie, doesn't know who Decker is. The writer reveals their reactions to Jo's bloody history rather than recapping a previous chapter.

Coincidentally, it turns out, Jackson was 'on manoeuvres on Dartmoor' and had to 'search' for Jo, after Decker murdered her family (410). The mystery increases as Louise speculates that Jo may be 'going after Andrew Decker' (410). She adds that 'a guy called Anderson' could be involved, if it is indeed a kidnapping (411). She calls Jackson, who is now in a front passenger seat, 'a waster', but he reacts by taking her hand in his (412). When she drops him off with Reggie, she reminds him that she doesn't 'want any amateur interference' with the case (413). This kind of comment is typical in the detective story genre.

Louise feels as if 'her brain' is 'fraying' as she 'should have taken that handbag off Reggie' (414). Louise takes good care of her partner, Marcus, dropping him at his house. She calls him 'Scout', which makes her sound like Atticus Finch talking to his daughter in 'To Kill A Mockingbird' (415). Perhaps like Atticus, she is meant to be the voice of reason and morality. This link subtly makes her seem a more likeable and loving character. Louise wants to go anywhere that isn't 'home' (416). We can sympathise with her predicament.

'A' Level Revision Notes – When Will There Be Good News
Chapter 31: Tribulation

This chapter seems to suggest there will be plenty of trials and tribulations for Reggie and Jackson, who are focal points.

Billy threatens Jackson with 'a nasty-looking penknife', which is quite a childish weapon that shows what a small-time gangster he is (417).

Billy is described as 'wild-eyed, like the horses in Midmar field', which suggests he cannot help his behaviour anymore than an animal can, especially under provocation which is the case when Sadie gets 'too close to them' (418).

This foreshadows what is about to happen as Sadie, who was mentioned in the description of Billy, now appears suddenly, coming to their rescue. Billy drops the knife and starts 'screaming' (419). He seems even less tough than before.

Jackson unexpectedly punches the dog, so it releases Billy. Jackson doesn't 'seem to care one way or the other' about Billy, so he lets him go when Reggie asks him to (420).

'A' Level Revision Notes – When Will There Be Good News
Chapter 32: High Noon

Like a cowboy movie, this chapter is entitled: 'High Noon'. It sounds like it will be a climactic point in the novel.

Jackson can't sleep, so he decides to search for 'livelier reading matter' than the Latin books that surround him (421). He can't 'find a readable book', so contents himself by going through Jo's handbag (422). For all of his soldier instincts, he is still taken by surprise when he hears 'a little, insistent voice' reminding him not to go 'anywhere without' her (423). Reggie's determination shines through.

Reggie takes control when they go to the Hunter's, as she instructs Jackson to 'follow' the 'Nissan Pathfinder' with Jo's Prius (424, 423).

The time setting is 5am 'on a winter morning', which makes it seem as if they are unlikely to succeed, as people are portrayed only grudgingly making their 'way through the early morning dark' (425). If Reggie and Jackson succeed it will be against the odds: a lucky shot in the dark.

'A' Level Revision Notes – When Will There Be Good News

After trailing the car, he insists that Reggie 'stay', while he sets 'off on foot' (426, 427). He spots Jo, looking like a 'dangerous avenging angel', 'veiled in blood' with a knife in her hand (428). She is portrayed here as an innocent victim, who has had the courage to fight back.

'A' Level Revision Notes – When Will There Be Good News

Chapter 33: La Regle De Jeu

The title means 'the rules of the game' in French, which makes us wonder who considers murder a game.

The narrative returns to Jo's perspective as we can feel her dream-like state, as she thinks of 'animals gnawing off a leg to escape' (429). Her survival instincts bring out the animal in her. Additionally, she cleverly insists on being 'friendly' to her captors, making it difficult for them 'to kill her' (430).

The setting where she finds herself is described negatively and poetically as 'nothing but brown fields, winter barren, lit by a bright, cold moon'. The moon seems to signify hope.

Jo thinks of Neil and how she sees him as 'Mars throwing his spear into the world' (432). This implies that she sees him as war-like and violent. She seems to be deluding herself as he is unlikely to be a rescuing hero.

Consequently, she takes matters into her own hands and resorts to violence to escape, when she jams a 'pen into' one of her captors' eyeballs as hard as she could'

'A' Level Revision Notes – When Will There Be Good News

(433). She seems surprised that she has managed to kill him so easily.

She expertly dispatches her other captor as well, the blood gushing as 'if she'd struck oil' (434). There is something disconcertingly violent about her actions, although we can assume it's borne of desperation and fear. Ironically, the baby laughs when he sees her kill their captors. Again there is something disconcerting about her behaviour, as she sings the nursery rhyme: 'Little Tommy Tittlemouse lived in a little house, he caught fishes in other men's ditches' (435). It could suggest insanity, or it could refer to the victory of the relatively diminutive against the odds.

'A' Level Revision Notes – When Will There Be Good News
Chapter 34: A Clean Well-lighted Place

The title refers to Hemmingway's short story of the same name. It seems to suggest the themes of death, futility and meaninglessness will come to the fore. Louise calls on Neil and asks him 'who' his 'friends are', to which he laughs 'grimly' (436). Louise speaks to him 'gently ', so has sympathy for him. He may be perceived as weak by the reader, as he bursts 'into tears' (437). She cannot believe that Neil put money before his family asking: 'You didn't sign everything over straight away' (438). He is portrayed unsympathetically, as he has put his business interests first rather than complying with the kidnappers' wishes to get his family back..

Louise is confronted by the sight of Jo 'sitting on the sofa', claiming she is suffering from 'temporary amnesia' (439). Louise is not so sure that is true.

Meanwhile, Karen brings Louise terrible news of Marcus's near death at the hands of David Needler. We are closer to Marcus's character than Alison's children, so his death has a stronger effect on readers. Meanwhile, it is made more poignant by the scene of 'non-denominational greenery to indicate Christmas' (440).

'A' Level Revision Notes – When Will There Be Good News

In response to Marcus's murder, Louise comments that 'fools rush in' (441). This seems harsh and unsympathetic, but is totally in character. However, she feels 'like a crazed Maenad', by she which effectively compares herself to the raving-mad followers of the god Dionysus in Greek mythology (441). This harsh comparison implies she has a guilty conscience about her secret feelings for Jackson.

Meanwhile, Louise tells a white lie to Marcus's mother, agreeing that he looks 'asleep' (442). This shows she does have a soft side to her.

'A' Level Revision Notes – When Will There Be Good News

Chapter 35: Sweet Little Wife, Pretty Little Baby

The title suggests it will be about Jo and the baby, of course. The sight of her 'covered in blood' is horrifying, and that effect is accentuated and made more real by the baby 'laughing' (443).

Jackson sets light to the building to get 'rid of the whole crime scene' and they leave as if they are 'walking out from hell' (444). This emphasises how good characters have had to fight evil with evil, or fire with fire.

Jo is determined to destroy the evidence, as she doesn't want her baby to be haunted by the past presumably, so asks Reggie to 'dispose' of their blood-soaked clothes (445). Reggie manages to take the evidence away without alerting the police, simply saying: 'Bye, folks' (446). Reggie is innocent enough to look at to get away with it.

'A' Level Revision Notes – When Will There Be Good News

Chapter 36: Great Expectations

The chapter is named after Charles Dickens's novel about Pip, who is initially threatened by a criminal but comes good anyway. Perhaps the same will be true of the characters in this chapter.

It begins with Jackson comforting a crying Louise, who is mourning the death of Marcus. She then shakes him off as if he is a 'nuisance' (447). She doesn't appear to be in touch with her true feelings.

Jackson heads home, his 'odyssey' finally over (448). This makes him appear like a traveling Homeric hero of Greek mythology. We wonder if there is more to come for him, though, as although he has waited for his wife at Heathrow, there is 'no sign whatsoever' of her (449). He feels 'sheep-dog like agitation' which implies he had some loyalty towards her still (450). He wonders if she arrived early so returns to their 'love nest' or 'little eyrie' in Covent Garden (451). This suggests that despite his hard exterior, Jackson is a true romantic to think of their flat in such terms. This is backed up by the poetic words that follow his discovery that Tessa is not there: 'Whither is thy beloved gone' (452).

'A' Level Revision Notes – When Will There Be Good News

He finds a dead body in his flat and he can 'smell it before' he sees it (453). This heightens the tension for the reader. He can't imagine ever returning to the flat and 'popping a can of beer in the same room where someone had, literally, blown their brains out' (454). He seems sensitive, given all the bloodshed he had experienced in his life.

Another mystery is given for him to solve, as it turns out his wife does not exist. 'No one' at the British Museum 'had ever heard of' her (455). All his money has disappeared too. He feels 'like the biggest fool ever' (456). He is 'too tired to rage', so accepts his fate stoically (456).

Unlike Pip in 'Great Expectations', Jackson has gone from riches to rags.

'A' Level Revision Notes – When Will There Be Good News
Part VI: Christmas

Chapter 37: A Puppy Is Just for Christmas

The title seems ironic, as puppies are not just for Christmas, according to animal rights organisations and other animal lovers.

However, someone has left a 'puppy, a tiny thing' outside Louise's house (459). Who put it there is yet another mystery for the reader to guess the answer to. She guesses it is Jackson, as the words 'faithful friend' makes her recognise his 'streak of sticky sentimentality a mile wide' (460).

She has that in common with him deep down, as she takes 'things people were supposed to have at Christmas' to Alison's (461). She has decided not to leave Patrick at Christmas as it would be 'cruel' (462). The news is cruel though, as Marcus's mother jumps 'off the North Bridge', so grief-stricken is she at her son's death (463).

Meanwhile, the saintly Jo is pictured positioning 'the white, top-of-the-tree angel' in her house (464). Louise

'A' Level Revision Notes – When Will There Be Good News

is starting to wonder how innocent Jo is in all of this, particularly in regard to Decker's suicide. However, Louise would 'rather fight with her than against her' (465). This shows how formidable Jo actually is. Unsurprisingly, she names her dog 'Jackson' after the man she loves (466). Louise is far more sentimental than she would care to admit. Again this could link to Dickens's sentimentality in 'A Christmas Carol'.

'A' Level Revision Notes – When Will There Be Good News

Chapter 38: The Rising of the Sun, the Running of the Deer

A lyric from the Christmas carol 'The Holy And The Ivy' is the title of this chapter. It seems as if some light is going to be shed on the mysteries, if the sun reference is anything to go by.

The setting is 'Christmas morning' and presents, as Reggie celebrates being with the Hunters (467). She wonders about Jackson's 'bounced' cheque and what that says about him, as it appears to her that he lied when he said was 'rich' (468). The writer uses dramatic irony to emphasise how even the honest are doubted.

Reggie contemplates the idea that 'death' absolves 'a lot of things', including 'the Musselburgh train crash' which the dead Ms MacDonald is not blamed for (469). She discreetly places Billy's heroine packets which she has found 'in the Loeb's secret hearts into the coffin with Ms MacDonald' (470). It shows how the past can be literally buried.

She wonders how Jo knows about Billy, as she feels sure 'she had never mentioned her brother to her' (471).

'A' Level Revision Notes – When Will There Be Good News

That is another mystery for the reader to consider. It seems Jo has decided to split with Neil who, unlike her, would not 'walk to the ends of the earth for someone' he 'loved' (472). It appears that Jo has finally realised that Neil is not good enough for her.

'A' Level Revision Notes – When Will There Be Good News

Chapter 39: God Bless Us, Every One

This quotation from Charles Dickens's 'A Christmas Carol' is spoken by Tiny Tim. It reminds us that the diminutive can tug on our heart strings the most and make us feel sympathy for them by being so grateful for what little they have.

The most diminutive character in the novel is Reggie, but the focus of the chapter is on her brother, Billy. He is wondering why Jo bought a 'Makarov' semi-automatic pistol from him (473). We are starting to realise, if we hadn't already, that Jo is far more violent that she seems on the surface.

The violence of society in general is emphasised by Billy swearing at an 'old drunk' who wishes him: 'Merry Christmas' (474). This makes whatever Jo has done seem less awful, as she is just a survivor of a violent world.

'A' Level Revision Notes – When Will There Be Good News

Chapter 40: Safely Gathered In

This chapter title refers to the harvest, presumably of dead bodies, which have littered the whole novel. It also could allude to religion.

The setting is 'Westminster Bridge', made famous by William Wordsworth's poem (475). Jackson hadn't expected to be in London at dawn on Christmas Day. Like the reader, Jackson's head is full of 'unanswered questions' (476).

Luckily, Jackson has had a stroke of luck as 'the sale of his French house was delayed', so money arrived in his 'account just before Christmas' (477). He is like a cat, it seems, as he always falls on his 'feet' (477). The theme of luck is explored through this pleasant surprise for Jackson.

Likewise, he thinks of Jo, whom he found in Devon all those years ago with 'not a scratch on her' (478). Like Jackson, Jo also had a stroke of luck, if we believe the story as to what happened to her family. Both characters are unified through the theme of luck.

'A' Level Revision Notes – When Will There Be Good News
Chapter 41: And Scout

The final chapter returns to Reggie, judging by the title. Although, 'Scout' is the name of someone's dog, according to Dr Hunter's story if we place greater significance to it then it seems to relate to Reggie's dog-like loyalty (479). Of course, the word 'scout' relates to observation and it is from Reggie's perspective that much of the plot is revealed.

Finally, 'the little cock sparrow' in the nursery rhyme seems to represent both of them, as they have triumphed in the face of adversity like the small bird in the poem (480). Additionally, Scout's surname in 'To Kill A Mockingbird' is Finch, so there another connection with a literary classic.

'A' Level Revision Notes – When Will There Be Good News
Useful information/Glossary

Allegory: extended metaphor, like the grim reaper representing death, e.g. Scrooge symbolizing capitalism.

Alliteration: same consonant sound repeating, e.g. 'She sells sea shells'.

Allusion: reference to another text/person/place/event.

Ascending tricolon: sentence with three parts, each increasing in power, e.g. 'ringing, drumming, shouting'.

Aside: character speaking so some characters cannot hear what is being said. Sometimes, an aside is directly to the audience. It's a dramatic technique which reveals the character's inner thoughts and feelings.

Assonance: same vowel sounds repeating, e.g. 'Oh no, won't Joe go?'

Bathos: abrupt change from sublime to ridiculous for humorous effect.

Blank verse: lines of unrhymed iambic pentameter.

Compressed time: when the narrative is fast-forwarding through the action.

Descending tricolon: sentence with three parts, each decreasing in power, e.g. 'shouting, talking, whispering'.

Denouement: tying up loose ends, the resolution.

Diction: choice of words or vocabulary.

Didactic: used to describe literature designed to inform, instruct or pass on a moral message.

Dilated time: opposite compressed time, here the narrative is in slow motion.

Direct address: second person narrative, predominantly using the personal pronoun 'you'.

Dramatic action verb: manifests itself in physical action, e.g. I punched him in the face.

'A' Level Revision Notes – When Will There Be Good News

Dramatic irony: audience knows something that the character is unaware of.

Ellipsis: leaving out part of the story and allowing the reader to fill in the narrative gap.

End-stopped lines: poetic lines that end with punctuation.

Epistolary: letter or correspondence-driven narrative.

Flashback/Analepsis: going back in time to the past, interrupting the chronological sequence.

Flashforward/Prolepsis: going forward in time to the future, interrupting the chronological sequence.

Foreshadowing/Adumbrating: suggestion of plot developments that will occur later in the narrative.

Gothic: another strand of Romanticism, typically with a wild setting, a sensitive heroine, an older man with a 'piercing gaze', discontinuous structure, doppelgangers, guilt and the 'unspeakable' (according to Eve Kosofsky Sedgwick).

Hamartia: character flaw, leading to that character's downfall.

Hyperbole: exaggeration for effect.

Iambic pentameter: a line of ten syllables beginning with a lighter stress alternating with a heavier stress in its perfect form, which sounds like a heartbeat. The stress falls on the even syllables, numbers: 2, 4, 6, 8 and 10, e.g. 'When now I think you can behold such sights'.

Intertextuality: links to other literary texts.

Irony: amusing or cruel reversal of expected outcome or words meaning the opposite to their literal meaning.

Metafiction/Romantic irony: self-conscious exposure of the devices used to create 'the truth' within a work of fiction.

Motif: recurring image use of language or idea that connects the narrative together and creates a theme or mood, e.g. 'green light' in *The Great Gatsby*.

'A' Level Revision Notes – When Will There Be Good News

Oxymoron: contradictory terms combined, e.g. deafening silence.

Pastiche: imitation of another's work.

Pathetic fallacy: a form of personification whereby inanimate objects show human attributes, e.g. 'the sea smiled benignly'. The originator of the term, John Ruskin in 1856, used 'the cruel, crawling foam', from Kingsley's *The Sands of Dee*, as an example to clarify what he meant by the 'morbid' nature of pathetic fallacy.

Personification: concrete or abstract object made human, often simply achieved by using a capital letter or a personal pronoun, e.g. 'Nature', or describing a ship as 'she'.

Pun/Double entendre: a word with a double meaning, usually employed in witty wordplay but not always.

Retrospective: account of events after they have occurred.

Romanticism: genre celebrating the power of imagination, spriritualism and nature.

Semantic/lexical field: related words about a single concept, e.g. king, queen and prince are all concerned with royalty.

Soliloquy: character thinks aloud, but is not heard by other characters (unlike in a monologue) giving the audience access to inner thoughts and feelings.

Style: choice of language, form and structure, and effects produced.

Synecdoche: one part of something referring to the whole, e.g. Carker's teeth represent him in *Dombey and Son*.

Syntax: the way words and sentences are placed together.

Tetracolon climax: sentence with four parts, culminating with the last part, e.g. 'I have nothing to offer but blood, toil, tears, and sweat ' (Winston Churchill).

ABOUT THE AUTHOR

Joe Broadfoot is a secondary school teacher of English and a soccer journalist, who also writes fiction and literary criticism. His former experiences as a DJ took him to far-flung places such as Tokyo, Kobe, Beijing, Hong Kong, Jakarta, Cairo, Dubai, Cannes, Oslo, Bergen and Bodo. He is now PGCE and CELTA-qualified with QTS, a first-class honours degree in Literature and an MA in Victorian Studies (majoring in Charles Dickens). Drama is close to his heart as he acted in 'Macbeth' and 'A Midsummer Night's Dream' at the Royal Northern College of Music in Manchester. More recently, he has been teaching 'A' Level and GCSE English Literature and IGCSE and GCSE English Language to students at secondary schools in Buckinghamshire, Kent and in south and west London.

Printed in Great Britain
by Amazon